Beautiful
New Hampshire

"Learn about America in a beautiful way."

Beautiful
New Hampshire

Concept and Design: Robert D. Shangle
Text: Paul M. Lewis

First Printing March, 1982
Published by Beautiful America Publishing Company
P.O. Box 608, Beaverton, Oregon 97075
Robert D. Shangle, Publisher

Library of Congress Cataloging in Publication Data
Beautiful New Hampshire
1. New Hampshire—Description and travel—1951—Views. I. Title.
F35.L48   917.42   81-9939   AACR2
ISBN 0-89802-289-4 (Hardbound)
ISBN 0-89802-288-6 (Softbound)

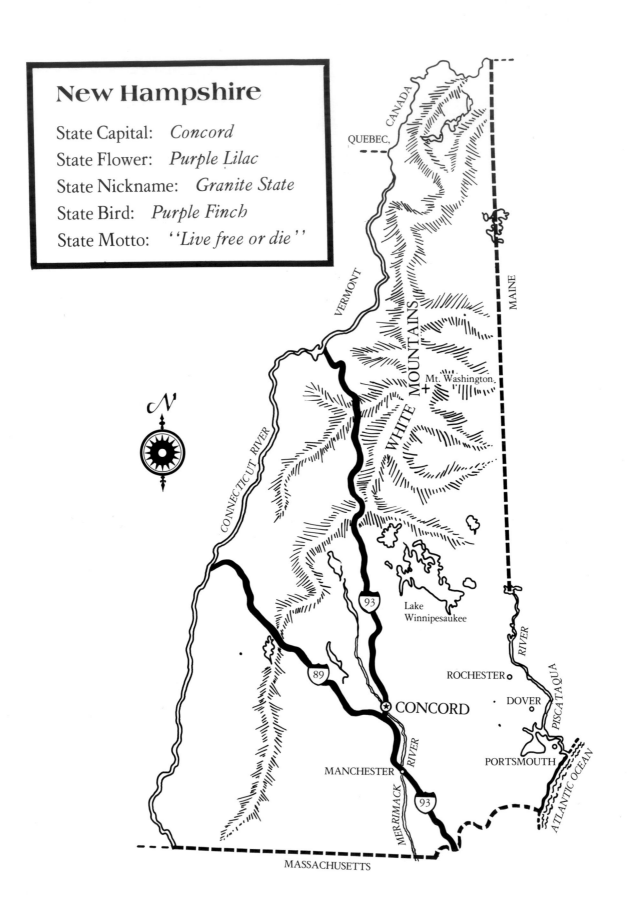

New Hampshire

State Capital: *Concord*
State Flower: *Purple Lilac*
State Nickname: *Granite State*
State Bird: *Purple Finch*
State Motto: *"Live free or die"*

Contents

Introduction

The United States is a very large, powerful, and awesome national entity. Some of its states have annual budgets bigger than those of many nations. The national stimulus for growth, expansion, and development has been created out of the determination and drive that was first displayed by early New England settlers who struggled to survive in this new land. But mere survival was a bit short of what the first Yankees had in mind for a goal. Their resourcefulness and restlessness soon sparked the irresistible drive west that finally reached across a whole continent. The American spirit of independent endeavor began in New England and it's still there. "Yankee ingenuity" is not just a catchphrase. After more than 300 years, there's no sign that the reservoir of this ineffable substance in the hearts and minds of New Englanders is in any danger of running dry. Although in the 20th century some other parts of the country have out stripped it in population and economic wealth, New England is still the lodestar. It's the spiritual leader and catalyst, which in many ways, guides the career of the entire nation.

New Hampshire is not large. But its 9,304 square miles assume many forms; its seasons bring with them a marvelous variety of weather. The beauty of its mountains and valleys, and rivers and lakes attracts a lot of tourists, and a lot of permanent residents, too. Some 800,000 persons now live in this triangular piece of New England, most of them in the cities of the south located near the 75-mile-wide base of the triangle. The big Connecticut River wriggles along the common border with Vermont. Counting the narrow northern tip, where the state shares a border with Canada, the western side measures 230 miles. That leaves the short coastal stretch and the long perpendicular line that is in common with Maine on the east: 180 miles.

New Hampshire's marvelous mountains, the Whites, are the tallest on the East Coast north of the Carolinas. They occupy the northern half, attaining their highest reach in the lofty and legendary Presidential Range. Mt. Washington's sometimes-stormy summit, 6,288 feet, tops all the others. In this mountain country are the headwaters of the Connecticut River on the west and of the Androscoggin River on the east. Population is still extremely light, leaving great chunks of unspoiled forest and wilderness. For many years the region has been a favorite haunt of hunters and fisherfolk; more recently, boating, skiing, and hiking have established its waters, slopes, and trails as prime attractions for a numerous East-Coast public seeking the outdoor experience in pristine surroundings.

Most of the farming in New Hampshire is done in the fertile Connecticut Valley. Some of the bigger towns along the lower river have developed as industrial centers and one, Hanover, is known before all else, as the home of Dartmouth College. The Merrimack Valley in south-central New Hampshire is another farm belt of some importance, although the valley's economic clout, these days, comes from the thriving and diversified industry that makes things go in Manchester, the state's biggest city, and in other big towns along the river.

The gods, who made New Hampshire, put in a lot of lakes. There are about 1,300 of them, big and little. Many of the biggest ones are concentrated in the lakes region, a zone generally east of the Pemigewasset River and south of the White Mountains. Giant Winnipesaukee, ''The Smile of the Great Spirit,'' is the centerpiece with other big lakes near it on all sides.

The southeast coastal plain is, of course, very important in New Hampshire's history. The towns of Dover, on the Piscataqua River; Portsmouth, on the seacoast at the mouth of the same river; and Rye and Hampton, farther down the coast, are where the first settlements were established. The southwest is old, too, in human terms. Keene is the big town here, right in the center of the forested hills and secluded dales typical of this ''Currier and Ives corner.'' These close-knit ridges and valleys hold on to their early-American charm, ornamented by Christmas-card villages more than 200 years old, each with its white, steepled churches. This is known as the Monadnock region, after the peak, 3,165 feet high, that dominates the southwestern high country.

There is, indeed, no part of New Hampshire that doesn't have its special appeal. That even includes the industrial centers. In this state folks have paid attention to keeping their working places comfortable to be in. As a result New Hampshire has developed into—or should I say, remained—one of the most satisfying environments this side of Paradise for the full life, the way people with a talent for living such a life define it.

P. M. L.

The South

To begin at the beginning, the first place to look at New Hampshire is where it began. That is on the coastal plane, on the snippet of seacoast the state manages to wedge in between the enormous hunks of land claimed by Maine and Massachusetts. This Atlantic Ocean frontage may be short on mileage, but it's long on significance. It was very early in the 1600s that the coastal waters of what is now New Hampshire were visited by explorers. One of these men was the Frenchman, Champlain. He entered the bay of the Piscataqua River in July of 1605 and is believed to have come ashore at the site of present-day Rye. Until the 1620s British colonization of the northern coast was more-or-less on hold, although Captain John Smith did some exploring in 1614 from Maine to Cape Cod. Through the efforts of Captain Smith and others, the Plymouth Company, in 1620, was granted the right to establish settlements on these shores and issue grants of land to individuals. One of those who received a grant from the Plymouth Council was David Thompson, a Scot. In 1623, with a small group of British colonists, Thompson came ashore at Odiorne's Point (Rye), near Portsmouth.

In the same year another party, led by the Hilton brothers, Edward and William, established an outpost eight miles up the Piscataqua River, at what is now Dover Point. Hilton Park, in present-day Dover, occupies the site of that settlement, once called Hilton Point. The Hilton and Thompson parties thus established themselves at almost the same time, although the formal grant of Hilton Point was not received from Plymouth until 1831. The Hilton and Thompson groups did not intermingle. Otherwise they might have agreed among themselves just who was first on the scene with a settlement. As a result there is still a lack of unanimity as to which town, Portsmouth or Dover, is ''first.''

Portsmouth was New Hampshire's center of government for a hundred years after receiving its grant as a township in 1631 from the Council of Plymouth. Piscataqua was the first name, then Strawbery Banke. The name, Portsmouth, was adopted in 1653 when the town was incorporated. Strawbery Banke, though, has endured into the present, from the days when the settlement at the mouth of the Piscataqua was in the front ranks of Colonial seaports. The name is descriptive of the strawberry-covered river banks in 1630. Now Strawbery Banke is the oldest part of Portsmouth, the downtown section by the river. Lately, as in other old cities of the East, a renewal project is bringing life to a ten-acre area that had fallen into decay. Thirty buildings of both historical and architectural interest are being restored. These include homes of merchants, captains, and craftsmen. Docks and other landmarks are getting a sprucing-up to at least an approximation of their ancient air.

The continuing preservation work involves many historic names and places. Daniel Webster, born in Franklin, New Hampshire, practiced law in Portsmouth around 1785, and the house where he lived still stands in Strawberry Banke. Some other historic places in this old riverside part of town are the Hiram Lowell & Sons Boat Shop, still in business since 1793; Prescott Park, with its Liberty Flagpole standing where the original Liberty Pole was raised by rebels in 1766 carrying a flag protesting British taxes (the Pole was a rallying point for many rousing revolutionary speeches); Point of Graves, the first cemetery, dating from 1671; and Josie Prescott Memorial Garden, a Colonial garden.

More historic landmarks have been restored to good health in other Portsmouth areas. They range in age from the late 17th century to the middle 19th. The Wentworth-Coolidge Mansion is noteworthy, begun in 1690 and added to thereafter. This immense (40-room) dwelling was the home of New Hampshire's first governor, Benning Wentworth, who ruled the colony from 1741 to 1767. The Governor John Langdon House, built by him in 1784, is one of the most ornate in town. The handsome detailing of its Corinthian columns and the rich carvings of its interior woodwork elicited the admiration of the important guests who were received there. The Warner House, named for Jonathan and Mary Warner, is the oldest brick house in town. It was a New England showplace when built in 1716, or thereabouts, and is a Registered National Historic Landmark. The Wentworth-Gardiner House (1760) is another handsome dwelling, featuring a paneled entrance flanked by columns and lavish interiors.

The list of old and elaborate buildings goes on, including many more residences of the great, or at least the wealthy, and several churches. St. John's Church, on a hill overlooking the river, was built of brick in 1807. It houses one of the four ''Vinegar Bibles,'' printed in 1717, known to exist in this country. These are rare and famous Bibles containing the misprint ''vinegar'' for ''vineyard'' in a page heading over a chapter in Luke. Other church treasures are an organ, built in England in 1710, and a bell, captured from the French at the siege of Louisburg in 1745 and recast by Paul Revere in 1807. Some of the most illustrious names in early American history are associated with the church, names such as Daniel Webster, Benjamin Franklin, and George Washington.

Portsmouth for many years has been a popular resort town. With the restoration of the beautiful historic homes and the rehabilitation of the wharf district over recent years,

Portsmouth is becoming even more of an attraction for visitors. Dover, the other contestant for "oldest," is much more of an industrial town. The state's "oldest permanent community" is only ten miles from the sea and benefits from inexpensive electric power supplied by the abrupt fall of the Cocheco River as it flows through town to join the Piscataqua. So water turns its wheels and salty air bathes its streets. The old town has many relics of its past, notably 18th- and 19th-century homes. Two of them are gathered into the Woodman Institute, an establishment with historical and natural history collections located on Central Avenue, the town's main street.

The Woodman House and the Hale House date from 1818 and 1813 respectively. The former is one of Dover's first brick buildings. The Hale House is a Federal-style mansion that for many years was the home of John Parker Hale, an illustrious New Hampshire legislator and diplomat who was also known as a great humanitarian and anti-slavery agitator. Another component of the Institute is the Damm Garrison House, a small log fort erected near the Cocheco River in 1675 by settler William Damm as protection against Indian attacks. Now, as a part of the Institute, the fort displays Indian artifacts, antiques, weapons, and armor. The Damm Garrison House is probably the best remaining example of such rare, one-story fortress cabins, with heavy, squared logs, ponderous doors, small windows, and an overhang around the entire building. More historical material is housed in the Institute's new Dunaway Hall.

The next two towns in historical order are Exeter (1638) and Hampton (1639). For a long time these original settlements were all there was to colonization of New Hampshire, the four towns being attached to the Massachusetts county of Norfolk for protection. Exeter's temporary union with the Bay Colony in no way softened the fiery spirit of independence that shaped its early radical history. Exeter's defiant stance toward authority got a running start from the Reverend John Wheelwright, one of the first settlers. Reverend Wheelwright had been banished from Boston for political and religious non-conformity. He was a brother-in-law of another religious radical, Anne Hutchinson, also a Bay Colony outcast. She fled south to Rhode Island. Wheelwright obtained a deed to land by the falls of the Squamscott River, below Great Bay, from the chief of the Squamscott tribe, a document preserved at Phillips Exeter Academy.

Today's beautiful, old, dignified, but still feisty, Exeter is known before all else as the home of that illustrious preparatory school for boys. Phillips Exeter's handsome 400-acre campus sets the community's architectural tone with its elegant Georgian Colonial and Classical buildings. When Exeter left off defying religious authorities, it turned to the business of political rebellion. That was as early as 1682, when the royal governor's tax collector was sent packing by the town's leading women. All through the decades leading up to the Revolution, Exeter paid scant respect to the edicts of the Crown, and by the time the war was imminent, the little town was awash with Patriots. It even became the New Hampshire capital during the war, because Portsmouth on the coast was infested with Tories.

Exeter, ten miles inland, has the salty tang of the sea in its veins and so does Hampton, the fourth and smallest of the first four settlements. But Hampton is right out there by the Atlantic and was, in former days, a substantial harbor town that sent out clipper ships along the sea lanes of the world. Today Hampton, like Rye and Wallis Sands north of it, is a coastal resort well patronized in the summer for its wide, white-sand beaches.

The Merrimack Valley

New Hampshire doesn't have sole claim to the Merrimack, but the river certainly is vital to the life of the state's biggest center of population. The Merrimack is water power incarnate. It flows south from the lakes region of central New Hampshire through the middle of the state's southern base. Here, along both sides of the valley, are the big towns —Concord, Manchester, Bedford, Merrimack, Nashua—and some 30 smaller communities, when added together, muster the economic muscle that makes New Hampshire work. Concord is the state capital, more than 30,000 strong. Downstream are Manchester and Nashua, the first and second cities in population.

Manchester is, indeed, a giant among the state's primarily small towns, with more than 98,000 in a cosmopolitan population mix. From the 1840s to the 1930s, the Amoskeag cotton mills, largest in the world, attracted workers of many ethnic backgrounds, especially French-Canadians, Greeks, and Poles. So this old Yankee city speaks several languages in addition to English. The French contribution has exerted a strong influence over every aspect of the life of the city: political, commercial, and social. In Manchester spoken French is almost as common as spoken English. Several of the city's mayors have been descendants of French-Canadians, the largest single group drawn to the city by the expanding textile and shoe industries, arriving in the middle of the 19th century and later during the Civil War years.

The Merrimack River cuts Manchester in two. Around the time of the Revolution, there were two villages, Goffe's Town on the west bank and Derryfield on the east. Before the end of the century, a bridge over the river connected them. The name of Manchester was adopted in 1810, suggesting the town's potential future as an industrial power, like its namesake city in Great Britain. This has, obviously, been the case, first with textiles and now with many diversified businesses and industries.

There is little evidence in the city today, of the early appearance of John Goffe and others who came north from Massachusetts in 1722 to set up housekeeping on Cohas Brook, at a falls on the Merrimack now named for Goffe. The Indians, of course, were there first, at another Merrimack cataract in the neighborhood. Later known as Amoskeag Falls, it was a favorite fishing ground, and the Penacook Indians had a large village on the east-bank bluffs. The library and museum of the Manchester Historic Association preserve the history of the city and nearby towns in their collections and displays, going back to the Indian days. The home of General John Stark, a small Colonial house built around 1737 and owned by the Daughters of the American Revolution, is still a part of the scene. Stark won distinction in the French and Indian Wars and especially, during the Revolution, at Bunker Hill and Bennington, Vermont. He lived in the Manchester house from 1758 to 1765, and was a resident of the city when he died, at age 93, having outlived all the Revolutionary generals except Lafayette.

Nashua is named for the Indians who once resided in the neighborhood and who called the early fur-trading post ''Watanic.'' The Nashuas probably would have had difficulty recognizing the tribal name from the ''Nash-a-way'' pronunciation given it by those later natives, the Yankees. Nashua developed early along diverse industrial lines, having the plentiful water power available not only of the Merrimack, but the Nashua River, too. The first settler arrived in 1656, and more in 1660. French-Canadians, Irish, Poles, Greeks, and Lithuanians have been the bulk of the population since Nashua began its surge toward 60,000 and beyond. Something of the town's rustic beginnings is remembered in the name of Salmon Brook, a little stream that is crossed by wide, straight Main Street. Salmon Brook once supported an abundant population of salmon, and although the streams hereabouts are still well endowed with fish, the greatest numbers of the finny kind are probably found in the big fish hatchery built by the federal government.

Concord is 18 miles upriver on the Merrimack from Manchester. The state capital has the additional distinction of being the home of the nation's largest legislature: 423 members. The Granite State's Capitol was built in 1819 of Concord granite, with an annex added in 1911. The classic, three-story structure, with columned central porch, arched second-floor windows, and octagonal dome, is set back from the street fronting a broad plaza shaded by big, old elms.

If Concord has an air of importance, it's entitled to it, for reasons other than being the state capital. The town's central position in the Merrimack Valley makes it a transportation crossroads, a circumstance that began a long time ago. Concord was a place established by a grant, in 1659. It wasn't until about 1727 that settlement began in earnest, on the fertile alluvial soil of the Merrimack's west bank. The Indians of the area had named the location Penacook, ''the crooked place,'' because of the twists and turns of the river at this spot. Those Indians were friendly to the new settlers, and the early town escaped most of the Indian troubles that were associated with other settlements. One of the town's famous and most enduring achievements was the Concord Coach. One of them is housed in the New Hampshire Historical Society's white granite museum-library near the State House. The Concord Coach was one of the keys to the opening of the West, because of its reputation as a reliable means of transport. Proof of the vehicle's durability is its use today in films about the Old West.

The Merrimack Valley is indeed one of America's most historic places, and certainly one of its most beautiful. The big towns on the river are just a part of the story. Elsewhere in the valley the landscapes are a scenic combination of hills and trees and streams, with here and there a charming old village that looks just right in its setting. The patented New Hampshire air, clean and bracing, is part of the livability factor. The town of Derry, east of the river, is part of the setting that lent itself to the poetry of Robert Frost, who lived here from 1900 to 1910 while he taught at Pinkerton Academy in Derry Village, a residential section. Frost's homestead, a one-man farm where he wrote many of his poems, is in the vicinity. Derry's long-running industrial career is symbolized by the Sawyer Mill, an up-and-downer aged 200 years and counting, one of the oldest sawmills in the Northeast.

The Connecticut Valley

The lower southwest corner along the Connecticut River is a region of gentle up-and-down scenery that has come to stand for the visual charm of old New England. Its atmospheric early American villages in settings of ponds, woods, and hills bring back a time when life's solid values seem, in retrospect, to have been more important than they are now. True or not, the "Currier and Ives corner" has undeniable appeal. This is the Monadnock region, for Mt. Monadnock, the highest (3,165 feet) of 15 or so high points scattered over the area. In the valleys, among the lakes, ponds, and meadows are a covey of little villages in various assortments of beautiful, charming, beauteous, or just plain pretty. One may be obliged to scale the heights of redundancy in speaking of them.

Fitzwilliam is one. Like many New England towns, it has a handsome, well-kept common, or village green, and some dignified and venerable public buildings, churches, and private dwellings, some of great age. Then there's Dublin and Hancock, Greenfield and Gilsum, Chesterfield, Ashuelot, Harrisville, Jaffrey, Mason, Milford, and Peterborough. All of them, and several more, have architectural features and historic connections that give them a rousing individuality of the sort that seems hard to find in our generally homogenized countryside.

Keene is *Numero Uno* among the lower Connecticut Valley towns. The modern industrial community is situated at the very heart of the Monadnock region. A population of more than 20,000 makes the wheels turn in a variety of concerns that turn out a lot of things, from shoes to machine tools, toys to textiles. The Keene main street may be the world's champion for wide streets: 172 feet. Other roads radiate from Keene to all points of Monadnock. One of them leads east for about 19 miles to Peterborough, nationally celebrated for its long-established Macdowell Colony, where the fine arts are well served during summer retreats in the woodlands. The colony was established from the date of its original grant. Since the early 1800s it has earned its livelihood as a cotton mill community. Manufacturers over the years have become more diversified, and in our era of active tourism, both winter and summer, Peterborough has become a flourishing resort town.

For all its cultural luster, Peterborough is not the only place in Monadnock where creativity finds an outlet. Swanzey Center, south of Keene, holds a summer drama revival, and more than ten towns over the region unite in a summer festival called "Music in Monadnock," featuring a series of 30 informal classical-contemporary concerts held in venerable and beautiful town churches and meeting houses. And over near Rindge and Jaffrey, the Cathedral of the Pines, an international, non-denominational outdoor shrine, combines natural and man-made art in two National War Memorials: the Altar of the Nation and the Memorial Bell Tower, honoring Americans killed in wars. The high-level views of mountains and lakes add a serene beauty to the shrine.

The culture capital of New Hampshire, and a lot more, would have to be Hanover, 62 miles up the valley from Keene on the Connecticut River. The Dartmouth-Lake Sunapee region comprises a distinct area in the west-central part of the state between the Merrimack and Connecticut rivers. Hanover shares some of this space with Lebanon and Claremont, two other medium-sized towns, and a numerous gathering of small communities that began to function, in most cases, more than 200 years ago. Hanover is actually on a plateau above and a little back from the river. Its main and almost sole reason for being is, and has always been, Dartmouth College. The liberal arts institution, now coeducational, has been the dominant factor in the affairs of the town ever since the college and the community came into existence, almost simultaneously. Hanover was settled in 1765. Dartmouth came to life four years later. It was named for the Earl of Dartmouth, who was one of the original trustees, and has become one of a very select group of the East Coast's blue-ribbon schools through the years.

From Hanover south through the Connecticut Valley is a scenic journey that can be taken on State Route 10. The short stretch (State Route 120) to Lebanon features the Connecticut River itself, with the highway high enough and near enough for allowing good viewing of the big waterway and its hilly, green banks. State Route 120 continues to Claremont, while Route 10 finds its way to Newport, about the same distance south and close to Lake Sunapee. The lake is the biggest of many lakes, ponds, and puddles in a region of the state whose cup runneth over with clear, pure, lovely, unpolluted water.

Interstate Highway 89 invades the Sunapee countryside, looking big and strange, stabbing through the close-knit hills and valleys. However, its presence seems of no great moment to the towns along its route, serenely unimpressed by roads built only to get from one point to another in as fast a time as possible. Old villages nearby, such as Croydon and Grantham, do what they've been doing since the middle of the 18th century, living a rich life in their rich valley and letting the world go rushing by, if it must.

Numerous other area towns fit into the "beautiful, old, and quiet" category, among them Orford, Lyme, Warner, Wilmot, and Washington. Orford is the farthest north of these, located along the Connecticut River in a hollow formed by the western ramparts of the White Mountains. This one-street town has an exceptional grouping of early houses, possibly the finest in the state, built in the period 1773-1839 and set on spacious, fenced grounds. Lyme, a few miles south, has fine river views and some fine old (and rare) carriage sheds along with its early homes and white church. Warner, Wilmot, and Washington sound like a trio of corporation lawyers but are really three towns set in idyllic woods, mountain, and pond country between Concord and Claremont. Warner and Wilmot, in addition, have close access to mountainous Rollins State Park and to Winslow State Park, where Mt. Kearsarge provides a 2,937-foot viewpoint. Washington is the first United States town named (in 1776) for George Washington, honoring the commander of the Continental Army.

Claremont, the big town that shares valley space near the western border, rises from the banks of the Sugar River where that stream enters the Connecticut River. The community's name, like those of so many towns hereabouts, honors a prominent 18th-century Englishman. Claremont was the English estate of Lord Clive, a friend of Provincial Governor Benning Wentworth. The town was settled in the 1760s and at the site of the 300-foot fall of the Sugar River provided plenty of water power for early grist- and sawmills. Smelters and textile mills were soon added to the industrial base. Paper making and machinery plants became part of the scene later in the 19th century, spurred by inexpensive power and an abundant labor supply. For all of its commercial prowess, Claremont has a tradition of interest in the arts, most especially music. Many of its residents, numbering about 14,000, are actively involved in the town's several musical organizations.

Dam near Concord

Lake Winnipesaukee

19

Scene near Durham

The White Mountains near Kancamagus Highway

Connecticut River
(Following pages) The White Mountains

Autumn scene near South Tamworth

23

Spring in Hollis

Little Lake Sunapee

Mt. Washington Hotel, Bretton Woods

28

Waterfalls at Jackson

Jackson

Intervale

Lake in the White Mountains

Linderhoff Village

View of Eaton Center and Crystal Lake

34

North Conway

Covered bridge at Conway

The countryside in winter

Lake in the White Mountains near Conway

Glen Ellis Falls
(Following pages) Lake Chocorua

Intervale

Little Lake Sunapee

Cathedral Ledge and Washington Valley

Swift River Covered Bridge

Washington Valley

Church at Sandwich Center

47

Crawford Railroad Station

48

The Swift River

Mt. Washington from Tasker Hill

50

Swiftwater Covered Bridge

Covered bridge in Conway

52

Cathedral Ledge, North Conway

North Wood Lake
(Following pages) Waterfall at Jackson

Covered bridge near Franconia Notch

55

Albany Covered Bridge

Lake near Claremont

Mt. Adams, Presidential Range

Lake at Rocky Gorge

61

Silver Cascade, Crawford Notch State Park

Covered bridge in Bath

The Lakes
and the Mountains

It seems almost unnecessary to talk about a lakes region in New Hampshire. The whole state could be called one. But there *is* a lakes region with such a concentration of lakes that one could travel almost all of it by boat. The area is generally in east-central New Hampshire, with no large towns except Laconia. It is just south of the White Mountain mass, and, indeed, would probably be known as hilly and mountainous country itself, were it not for all those lakes. There are more than 100 of them, including Winnipesaukee, the biggest of all. The neighborhood near this inland sea accommodates several other good-sized ones: Squam, Winnisquam, Wentworth, Ossipee, and Newfound.

Lake Winnipesaukee has an extensive history in human events to go with its long shoreline. Today the big glacial lake and its shores are counted among the prime vacation resorts of New England. Anything that's done in, on, or near water is done there, including fishing, boating, swimming, camping, and even lake tours on a big cruise ship. It's not really so different from the time of the vacationing Indians, who probably did many of the same things, even to lake cruises. But what they probably did best was fish. And they didn't leave it to chance, as the name Weirs Beach suggests. Weirs Beach, the chief resort on the lake shore, is located at the narrow southwest outlet of the lake. It was formerly known as The Weirs, for the fish weirs (nets) placed in the narrow channel by Indians, for longer than anyone can tell.

There's a big boulder at the edge of the swimming beach nearby. Known as Endicott Rock, it marks the place of farthest penetration in the area by English explorers in 1652, sent out by the Massachusetts Bay Colony. Endicott Rock is inscribed with the names of the explorers and is named for John Endicott, the governor who sent them out on their exploration. The big rock is now protected as a National Historic Site, but nature will have her way, and those early carvings on the boulder are becoming less of a presence with each passing year.

The lake is enormously complex. The shoreline is highly irregular along the 22-mile length, with several arms, or bays. The width ranges from one to ten miles, and the deepest water is more than 300 feet. In a basin that would be a complication of hills and valleys if no lake were there, the islands are numbered in the hundreds, many of them quite large and habitable. The long Indian name *winnipesaukee* is suitably intricate for such a lake. The present spelling took a state legislative act to establish, after the name went through more than 130 other spellings. The number of legends about the name and its meaning almost equal the variations in spelling.

One story has to do with the establishment of peace between two warring lake tribes, when the daughter of one chieftain was given to a rival brave. Reportedly, the lake began to glow as the young couple paddled across it, and the father of the bride declared the body of water would thence be knowns as Winnipesaukee, ''the smile of the Great Spirit.'' Other meanings are claimed for the name, but this is one of the more satisfying.

Weirs Beach is backed up by Laconia, which is spread around three other lakes besides Winnipesaukee. The town has shoreline on Paugus, Opechee, and Winnisquam lakes, strung out southwest of the big lake. The community has the best of both worlds economically: diversified industry and a flourishing resort trade. Laconia really should be good at what it does; the town has been working at it since 1777. Some of the other lakeside towns are even older. Wolfeboro, on the hilly southeast shore, was granted in 1759. It got an early boost toward settlement when Colonial Governor John Wentworth built a summer home there in 1768. Moultonborough is on a northeast arm of the lake and has been in business since 1763. Another lake town is Meredith, set out in a little hollow on the west side between little Lake Waukewan and an arm of Winnipesaukee, up the road from Weirs Beach. It dates from 1748.

New Hampshire's second largest lake has a little name: Squam. It occupies a plush setting just over Red Hill at the north end of Winnipesaukee. Squam Lake has received an extra dose of glamour from nature, with shores of dense forest backed by high, green hills. Still farther in the background are some of the southern White Mountain peaks. Visually, autumn is one of the most awesome times of the year around the lake, when the nippy New England weather turns the foliage into blazing splashes of color.

Another pristine body of water among the big lakes is Newfound, all by its lonesome across the Pemigewasset River a few miles west. One of the delightful scenic drives so abundantly available in New Hampshire is along the west shore from the Bristol vicinity at the south end to Hebron, a beautiful, old village on the north. Hebron lies along the Cockermouth River, which flows into Newfound Lake. To get there the river squeezes through a deep cleft, carving some whimisical shapes into the rocks in its 30-foot fall.

The White Mountains

At the northern edge of the lakes region, near where the White Mountains start to mean business, are the Sandwiches, very appealing little resort villages in various versions of Sandwich, including East, North, Center, and just plain Sandwich. Many illustrious names have been associated with Sandwich over the years, as original grantees, as residents, or as summer visitors. One of the latter, Cornelius Weygandt, a Philadelphian by birth and occupation and a New Englander by adoption, wrote lovingly of the Sandwich district in his atmospheric book, *November Rowen,* published in 1941. Another name closely linked with the old (circa 1763) community is that of John Phillips, founder of the famed academies at Exeter, New Hampshire, and Andover, Massachusetts, that bear his name. Phillips acquired proprietary rights to Sandwich in 1770.

This is the Bearcamp River country of the White Mountain fringes, celebrated in poetry of John Greenleaf Whittier. The little stream flows out of the mountains and east through the hills to Ossipee Lake near the Maine border. The encircling mountains—the Squam and Sandwich ranges on the north, the Ossipees to the east, and Red Hill, south —reach from 2,000 through 4,000 feet in altitude, and give the Sandwich country some of that idyllic isolation provided by northern New Hampshire's mountain greenery. One of those southern peaks, in the Sandwich Range, is Mt. Chocorua, named for a mighty Indian chief. Chocorua rises to 3,475 feet, and its glamorous pyramidal shape is clothed in thick forest. It is possibly the most popular hiking mountain of all, with many trails to the top, where the view of this beautifully rumpled land is more than marvelous. The view at the bottom of the mountain isn't bad, either. Especially the view from little Lake Chocorua under the southern flank, lying still in the quiet of the thick pine forest around it, and reflecting the tall silhouette of the mountain on its silver surface.

The White Mountain wilderness has a small ''w'' because it is not an upper-case Wilderness. Not official, that is—so designated and without human habitation or uncrossed by roads. However, that is really a technicality, because the 1,200 square miles occupied by the Whites in northern New Hampshire are as totally beautiful as any place you'll see on today's earth. Most of the ranges that are grouped under this name are in the White Mountain National Forest.

The Presidential Range presides at the heart of this mountain mass, tallest of them all. The Presidentials stretch in two curving ridges from the northeast to the southwest. At the mid-point of the two curves is Mt. Washington, whose 6,288-foot height gives it leave to look down on all the others. From the north to the south end of the range, the peaks are Madison, Adams, Jefferson, Clay, Washington, Monroe, Eisenhower, Pierce, Jackson, and Webster, the last one being the lowest at 3,896 feet. Their summits are deprived of trees, because the harsh weather regime of the upper levels puts the timberline at about 4,000 feet. This is especially true of Mt. Washington, with a reputation for the world's most violent weather. Shrieking winds from the North Atlantic have been recorded at the peak's weather station (in April 1934) at 231 miles an hour, a world record. Temperatures get as low as minus 49 degrees Fahrenheit, and the annual average is below freezing.

Many climbers over the years have perished in the lofty mountain's merciless winter weather. The bare granite upper slopes get 15 feet of snow a year. Miraculously, some life does exist on these arctic heights, notably some unique varieties of alpine plants. To help other life reach the top, there's a road and a cog railway, which seems like a lot of fuss to get someplace where you may be in some danger of being blown into the next state. But as that peerless phrase maker P. T. Barnum once said, the view up there is "the second greatest show on earth." Mr. Barnum wasn't exaggerating. When the clouds part enough to allow it, the eye can reach out into 150 miles of natural glory.

The White Mountains are just as inspiring when admired from the bottom side. That's because the valleys are only 500 to 1,000 feet above sea level, leaving the mountains to rise in a grand, unbroken sweep from the surrounding countryside. There are many ranges besides the Presidentials, which are separated from the others by deep valleys and by narrow cuts called notches (the same as gaps or passes in other parts of the country). There's Pinkham Notch on the east, Crawford Notch on the southwest, Jefferson Notch on the west, and two valleys, Jefferson and Randolph, on the north. Nowadays, highways follow stream courses around some of the White Mountain ranges. State Highway 16 cuts between the Presidentials and another long range to the east across Pinkham Notch. On the west side of Crawford Notch is a broad highland called the Pemigewasset wilderness and west of that the tall Franconia Range, with Mt. Lafayette, the highest peak (5,299 feet) in the middle. Franconia Notch is on the west side of these mountains.

There are nine notches in the White Mountain system, all magnificently deep and grand, containing the sparkling streams that contribute their flow to mighty New England rivers, such as the Connecticut and the Merrimack. Rushing brooks tumble down the mountain sides and through the forests in murky torrents and misty waterfalls. Three of the notches—Pinkham, Crawford, and Franconia—are especially memorable for a number of reasons. History has a lot to do with the case. They function, too, as gateways to some of the region's most desirable wild sanctuaries.

To alter a famous Shakespearean superlative, Pinkham Notch might be called "the most grandest cut of all," were not Crawford and Franconia equally deserving of extravagant descriptives. Pinkham, being next to the superlative Mt. Washington, has a certain built-in glamour. The little all-season resort of Jackson, lying high and snug at the southern end of the notch, is one of New Hampshire's premier attractions for skiers and vacationers. The notch and the village are deep in the mountain heartland's most showy scenery. Peaks rise up in every direction within a ten-mile radius of Jackson. Trails and ski lifts to mountain tops bring an extra dimension to the art of wilderness watching. The top of Wildcat Mountain, across the notch from Mt. Washington, is a front-row viewpoint for gazing at the big peak, and at others in the vicinity.

Jackson is also a handy outpost for visiting Crawford Notch on the Saco River, at the south end of the Presidentials. The notch is named for Abel Crawford, who ran a pioneer mountain inn with his family, starting in the 1790s. Crawford also blazed trails up the mountains and guided hikers to surrounding peaks. Among the events in the history of the notch is a memorable tragedy that occurred late in the summer of 1826, after some unusually prolonged hot and dry weather. A deluge on the night of August 26 set off an avalanche that thundered down a 2,000-foot-high bluff, at the base of which was the farmhouse of Samuel Willey and his family of six. Alerted by the sound of the approaching landslide, the Willeys ran from their house to what they thought was a safe spot. The slide did not touch the house, dividing, miraculously, before it reached that spot. The place where the family sought shelter was buried under the enormous moving mass. The tragedy of the Willeys was immortalized in a story by Nathaniel Hawthorne. The site of their house is marked in Crawford Notch State Park.

Franconia Notch is a steep, eight-mile-long cut located in the western side of the Whites. The flashy little Pemigewasset River runs through the gorge over rocks of assorted tints, accounting for a fair share of the beauty that has made the area a tourist attraction for more than 100 years. The notch has some unusual natural features, including the Old Man of the Mountains, a rock profile of a human face. The formation was the inspiration for Hawthorne's story, ''The Great Stone Face.'' Faces tend to fall as they get older, but this one is still high up there on its stormy mountain perch, with the help of an anchor-iron ''face lift.'' The Flume Gorge is another curiosity of the notch, discovered in 1803. It was formed in some distant era when the rocks in the neighborhood were moving and shaking and melting. The Flume was created by the gradual erosion of a lava dike formed of material pushed up through the granite. After thousands of years the narrow, perpendicular chasm has been widened by weather and water.

The primary roads through the White Mountain notches and valleys have been in place, in various forms, for a long time. A more recent one is the Kancamagus Highway, a state secondary road through a previously inaccessible mountain wilderness. The 34-mile route connects Conway on the east side with Lincoln, where the upper Pemigewasset flows south through the western mountain area. Campgrounds, scenic areas, and picnic grounds are scattered along the highway. The powerful-sounding name of Kancamagus, by the way, honors the man who was chief of the Penacook Indians in the late 17th century, when that confederacy dominated much of the New Hampshire territory.

The mountains extend north into the narrow tip of New Hampshire, beyond the main body of the national forest. This is as wild and unspoiled an area as any, all the way north to the Connecticut Lakes chain in the very top of the tip, where the Connecticut River begins its long meander through New England on to Long Island Sound. The powerful Androscoggin River rises in Umbagog Lake astride the Maine-New Hampshire border. The stream flows south, a few miles in from that border, and is the main reason why Berlin, the big paper-making town in these parts, got that big. Berlin's 15,000-plus residents are dependent on a 400-foot fall (in six miles) of the river when it passes through the town vicinity. In Berlin the Androscoggin derives additional power from compression between narrow walls of rock.

Berlin is a sports center, too, with encircling mountains providing plenty of slopes for practitioners of *le ski*. Berlin has things pretty much to itself between here and the Canadian border. The few other towns are small and scattered, connected by the few highways that penetrate the tip. One of those roads joins Gorham and Lancaster. The former town commands the northern approach to the Presidential Range at the confluence of the Androscoggin and Peabody rivers four miles south of Berlin. Lancaster, located west of Berlin, is a Connecticut Valley farm community settled in 1764. The village has a very wide main street with many fine old houses built before the 1800s. It also has some fine old views east to the Presidentials.

Dixville Notch is in the very middle of all this, the farthest north of the White Mountain passes. At an altitude of 1,871 feet, it is a rugged and narrow passageway hemmed in by mountains and crossed by State Route 26. The road is the only cross-state highway in the far northern part, connecting the towns of Errol and Colebrook and passing through wild fishing, hunting, and logging country. The area has been found to be pollen-free, or nearly so, making it a happy hunting ground for the allergy-prone among hikers, campers, and all other brands of nature lovers. Tiny Errol is in superlatively scenic lake-and-hill country, centered on big, wild, and woodsy Umbagog Lake. A 13-mile scenic road from Errol skirts the lake, exploring some of this grand isolation, where the bald eagle and osprey, among other endangered species are reported to be taking up residence.

Pittsburg is the farthest north of the towns. It stands on a bluff above the Connecticut River, a frontier town that preserves a frontier air. Three of the state's many covered bridges are nearby. The river receives its first infusion of water from the three Connecticut Lakes and Lake Francis, which lie one after the other in a northeasterly curve all the way up to where the United States becomes Quebec. The only people noises here are produced, in the warm season, by fishermen, hunters, and campers in a still, small corner of the country where events move on nature's scale of time.

Photo Credits

JAMES BLANK—*page 17; page 21; page 22; page 23; pages 24-25; page 27; page 32; page 34; page 38; page 43; page 44; page 46; page 49; page 51; page 54; page 58; page 59; page 62; page 63; page 64.*

COLOUR LIBRARY INTERNATIONAL—*page 18.*

JOHN HILL—*page 19; page 20; page 28; page 29; page 30; page 33; page 35; page 36; page 39; page 45; page 47; page 48; page 53; page 55; pages 56-57; page 60.*

FRED SIEB—*page 26; page 31; pages 40-41; page 42; page 50; page 52; page 61.*

HANS WENDLER *page 37.*

Color Separations and Printing
by
Universal Color Corporation
Beaverton, Oregon

Beautiful America Publishing Company

The nation's foremost publisher of quality color photography

Current Books

Alaska	Maryland	Oregon Vol. II
Arizona	Massachusetts	Oregon Coast
Boston	Michigan	Oregon Country
British Columbia	Michigan Vol. II	Pacific Coast
California	Minnesota	Pennsylvania
California Vol. II	Missouri	Pittsburgh
California Coast	Montana	San Diego
California Desert	Montana Vol. II	San Francisco
California Missions	Monterey Peninsula	San Juan Islands
California Mountains	Mormon	Seattle
Chicago	Mt. Hood (Oregon)	Tennessee
Colorado	Nevada	Texas
Dallas	New Jersey	Utah
Delaware	New Mexico	Utah Country
Denver	New York	Vancouver U.S.A.
Florida	New York City	Vermont
Georgia	Northern California	Virginia
Hawaii	Northern California Vol. II	Volcano Mt. St. Helens
Idaho	North Carolina	Washington
Illinois	North Idaho	Washington Vol. II
Indiana	Ohio	Washington, D.C.
Kentucky	Oklahoma	Wisconsin
Las Vegas	Orange County	Wyoming
Los Angeles, 200 Years	Oregon	Yosemite National Park

Forthcoming Books

Alabama	Kauai	Oahu
Arkansas	Maine	Phoenix
Baltimore	Maui	Rhode Island
Connecticut	Mississippi	Rocky Mountains
Detroit	New England	South Carolina
The Great Lakes	New Hampshire	South Dakota
Houston	North Dakota	West Virginia
Kansas		

Large Format, Hardbound Books

Beautiful America	Beauty of Washington	Lewis & Clark Country
Beauty of California	Glory of Nature's Form	Western Impressions
Beauty of Oregon	Volcanoes of the West	

For a complete product catalog, send $1.00.
Beautiful America Publishing Company
P.O. Box 608
Beaverton, Oregon 97075